Haiku Poems of a
Woman's Journey

By

Virginia R. Degner

Dedication

I dedicate this book of Haiku poems to my sister,
Brenda MacIntosh Bigongiari

Acknowledgments

With thanks and love to my children, Barbara, Karyn, Michael, and to Terry, Victoria, and Roy, who love my children, and to my grandchildren, Brandon, Treves, Taylor and Camille, whose lives have touched mine and taught me so much about what it means to be a family. With special thanks and love to my husband, Duane, who has always encouraged my dreams.

Foreword

American poet Mary Oliver characterizes the poetic mind by saying, "A mind that is lively and inquiring, compassionate, curious, angry, full of music, full of feeling, is a mind full of poetry." My Haiku poetry book contains many of these qualities and more. With passion, intensity, longing, and humility I sought to convey my desires and wishes, my losses and gains, my love and its' nemesis in pure poetic verse. I chose to structure the poems in the traditional form of Haiku because I found the simple three line verse to be compact, contained and yet very profound. I have been included in seven anthologies to date, of poetry that emphasis traditional poetic form.

I hadn't discovered Haiku poetry until early this year when my friend Bonnie Best introduced the form to me. After her brief instruction of the form of five sylables for the first line, seven sylables for the second line and five sylables for the third line, I went home and tried my hand at them.
I immediately found the exercise extremely satisfying and enlightening as to what my stream of consciousness was revealing to me.

I worked for many years as both a newspaper columnist and later I obtained my Master's degree in clinical psychology. I worked as a social worker and a therapist until my retirement six years ago. As a professional in the mental health field I struggled with my desire to be traditional with my clients and also to be creative with them. Within a simple poem form such as Haiku I have found to be very healing and I encourage anyone who is struggling with their life issues, which is most of us, to give the form a try to help them seek enlightenment and healing.

I do not think that this will be the only work necessary for someone who has deep seated, life impacting issues that are hindering their progress toward wholeness and well being, and I encourage them to seek counseling or psychiatric help if needed. However I do feel it can be a wonderful resource for people who seek to use Haiku as a way to get in touch with their inner self.

- Virginia Degner
Castro Valley, California
   June 3, 2013

A double rainbow
A wondrous mysterious,
Gift of luck and joy

The Blue Lake pole beans

stretch high, touch the sky, sun kissed

Little pods peek through leaves.

New Birth

The baby boy sleeps
in sweet innocence, brings joy.
Nature's gift endures.

It was mama's face
Looking at me smiling sweet!
Eyes hooded from sun.

My heart is mended
Stitches even and careful
Beating like bird wings

Little girl jump, run, play!
Spring blooms, urge life a~new
Red, yellow, pink, blue!

The calm sea is smooth
Sunrays shimmer in the swells
Time for peace and joy.

Friends stay close to me
Connects our life memories,
Like birds gathering.

Soar like an eagle
Gliding through sunlit shadows
Royal bird brings joy!

The child waits in vain.
All love is blocked, resisting
God forgives fox?

Dove remains silent,
No one reaches out in love.
Why is it so hard?

Fifty three years wed
is mysterious for sure.
Our season winter.

Storm at sea rages,
Its power unleashed at night,
It rocks our ship bed.

Peace, joy, love, power
I savor the sun setting
My creator reigns!

Love's commandment
The Dove cooed quietly, sweet.
Message of love sent.

Deep blue lake water
Clears the mind, quiets body.
Rejoice in the sun.

I open to love
As the butterfly searching
kisses the flowers.

Dawn is here, I wake.
Feel the sunshine warming me.
Air circles around.

My breath is living.
Makes circles around me,
like bees buzzing.

Gold hoop earrings shine,
bright gold, fresh from rivers deep.
Lovely, delight, joy!

Time to think an write.
Sit within the garden gate.
Listen to birds sing.

Walking at the lake,
birds fly over, soaring high.
Early morning peace.

Warm hands hold teacup
Healing tea fills my body
I hug the sunshine.

I soar like eagles.
Second half of life delights
Nourishes my soul.

Geese fly over me,
I feel the wind of their wings.
I duck in delight!

My poetry speaks,
Like water flows in a stream,
Gives voice to thought.

Cherish the children,
who run like the windswept leaves.
God's new beginning's.

I miss my children,
Scattered by the winds of life.
They regroup in mind.

My books leave my mind;
we connect through page of words,
like birds chattering.

My children's nature
is like butterflies: freedom,
to choose their landings.

My life is calm now,
no whirlwinds of storm blowing.
Just peace and quiet.

I'm free of working.
Like the woodpecker's pecking.
Free to think and be.

I wish for peace, love.

To share the sunshine with you

To walk together.

What is my purpose?
Nourish and love Your children?
Enjoy Your earth, sky?

Pancakes, bacon, juice!
Play thirty six holes of golf!
Sunshine, sharing, fun!

New day dawns awake!
Listen to the rooster's crow!
Listen to my heart!

Dark night, moon shadows.
Slip into dream world and peace.
Awake to sun, joy!

Walking with my friend
round the lake's silver waters.
We chatter an dream.

We walk on white sand
together yet apart, love
Gods gift of time thrills.

Sharing time with friends
in joyful conversation.
Sitting on a rock!

Calm my restless soul.
I sit on my garden bench
God's flowers soothe me.

Lovely eagle soars,
high above the bright blue lake.
Grateful for new day.

Its nice sitting close,
watching the brook bubble,
we share harmony.

I enjoy sunshine.
I prepare for abundance.
Live with gratitude!

The woman whispers,
be yourself, free yourself, now!
Like the hummingbird?

A walk in nature.

Eases me, calms my mind, heals me.

Sunshine warms my soul!

The double rainbow
kissing the sky, delights me!
Mysterious! Joy!

A child leaves its home,
The baby bird flees its nest.
Looks forward not back!

My garden earth clings to the
shovel, roots and worms.
I breathe the earth's scent!

Spider's are artists!
They spins their web like writers.
Never knowing the end!

I rejoice the dawn!
As sun reaches up so high,
from its bed of night.

Bold little Robin!
Plucks the worm from the soil.
Feeds her baby birds!

Take heart! God is near.
In the murmur of the bee,
As it drifts unseen.

I hear the clip, clip,
as my husband's clippers train
the tree's wild branches.

I visit the seashore.
The seals peeked above the waves.
Barked hello to me!

Spring's early this year.
savor the warm breezes!
Push winter away!

Butterflies frolicked,
Among roses wet with dew
Flying close to me!

The moon this dark night,
summoned by the earthly tides.
Soothes me to sweet dreams!

How the Robins sing,
In the garden damp with dew.
As the sun breaks morn!

The mermaids swam up
through the deep green sea water.
Their eyes stared at me.

My discordant mind.
I have no right to impose
on my friend's sunshine.

Its easy to be nice
when life flows like a slight breeze.
Hard when my joy flees.

Our life is too short
to be spent nursing anger.
Choose joy with sunshine!

The geese wings brush air,
high above me, reach the sky.
I yearn to follow!

The waves kiss my feet,
swirls water over my toes.
Brings me smiles to share.

Years of studying Jung,
archetypal concepts of mind.
Like clouds in the sky.

To dream your future,
laying in the grass, bees buzz
Dream on little one!

Images and feelings.
Reflections in lake water,
Frees my conscious mind.

The beach, warm sunshine,
gentle breeze, nudge my spirit.
Laughter feeds my soul.

Thin crust pizza yum!
A crisp green salad to share.
Lovers snuggle close!

The seaweed snake- like
slinks across the sandy shore,
to another place.

Pills, pills, daily pills!
I'd rather run on the beach,
than take daily pills.

Friends gather for lunch.
Chatter and catch up with news.
Like magpies in trees!

The moon shines brightly.

A garden of rich delights.

Beckons man to come.

A joy filled Christmas!
As cold winds of winter blew,
The fireplace warms us!

Expecting my babe.
It was our first Christmas eve,
As the wild wind blew.

My pear tree fruit grows
From tiny bud to lush fruit.
Nature's abundance.

California hills,
mark the San Andrea's fault.
May the luck prevail!

The hills caress me.
The lake and rivers bless me.
California gold!

Love one another!
So simple, so hard to do!
My free spirit soars like doves!

The night was dazzling!
Crisp, cold wind swirled around me.
Like angels dancing.

Sky like black velvet.
Sprinkled with stars, galaxies,
dazzles, cold, delights

Lady in attic
Sifts through her past memories.
Her mind soars like wind!

The airplane flies high.
Like an eagle after prey.
Its' wings whisper "bye"!

Slow down, take your time.

Savor the sunshine, so warm.

Savor, days gone by.

I walk round the lake.
Where the reclusive crane lives.
Enjoying the day!

I walk through the house,
Like a bird making its nest.
Secure, happy, yes!

Ode to bananas,
a yellow perfect fruit!
Nature's surprise gift!

The phone rings three rings,
It's my child, voice laughing.
Like the songbird sings!

A Mother's Day joy!
Natures great reward, new birth!
Like the sparrow's chick!

Social Media!

Instant communication!

Twitter's like bird chirps!

Giant sea turtles.
Spellbound I watch them swimming.
They restore my peace.

The tiny seed sprouts,
Into a tomato plant.
God's generous gift!

When I feel stressed,
I walk through the garden gate,
into peace and calm.

Praise for the woodlands
prairies and lakes, I seek peace,
and restore my soul.

It would be my wish
to sail the open sea ways
riding the waves joy!

Day dawns cool, cloudy.
We sip tea at the table.
Peace and love warm us.

Day's over, night near
I rejoice in the shadow.
The promise is here!

Made in the USA
Charleston, SC
31 July 2013